WORLD HABITATS

ISLANDS

Rose Pipes

RSVP

RAINTREE STECK-VAUGHN
PUBLISHERS
A Steck-Vaughn Company

Austin, Texas

Published by Raintree Steck-Vaughn Publishers,
an imprint of Steck-Vaughn Company

A ZOË BOOK

Editors: Kath Davies, Pam Wells
Design & Production: Sterling Associates
Map: Sterling Associates
Design Management: Joyce Spicer
Electronic Production: Scott Melcer

Library of Congress Cataloging-in-Publication Data

Pipes, Rose.
    Islands / Rose Pipes.
       p.   cm. — (World habitats)
    "A Zoë book"—T.p. verso.
    Includes glossary and index.
    Summary: Introduces some notable islands around the world, including
Madagascar, Hawaii, and South Georgia.
    ISBN 0-8172-5009-3
    1. Islands — Juvenile literature.   [1. Islands.]   I. Title.   II. Series: Pipes, Rose.
World habitats.
GB471.P66   1999
577.5'2 — dc21   97-46757
                                                     CIP   AC

Printed in Hong Kong by Midas Printing Ltd.
Bound in the United States
1 2 3 4 5 6 7 8 9 LB 02 01 00 99 98

Photographic acknowledgments

The publishers wish to acknowledge, with thanks, the following photographic
sources:

The Hutchison Library / Timothy Beddow 13; / Bernard Regent 21; Impact Photos / Geray
Sweeney 6; / Piers Cavendish 7, 15, 16; / Clip Clap 8; / Dominic Sansoni 19; NHPA / Jean-
Louis Le Moigne - cover inset tr; / Eric Soder 11; / Nigel J.Dennis 12; / David Middleton 17; /
Stephen Krasemann 23; South American Pictures / Robert Francis 4; / Tony Morrison 9; Still
Pictures / Don Hinrichson - cover background; / Mark Carwardine - cover inset bl; / Andy
Crump 18; / Alan Watson 22; TRIP / M.Nichols 10; / H.Rogers 14; / A.Tovy 20; /
D.Houghton 24; / John Gollop 25; Woodfall Wild Images / J. & E.Forder - title page; / Inigo
Everson 26, 27, 28; / Tom Murphy 29.

The publishers have made every effort to trace the copyright holders, but if they
have inadvertently overlooked any, they will be pleased to make the necessary
arrangement at the first opportunity.

Contents

All the words that appear in **bold** are explained in the Glossary on page 30.

What and Where Are Islands?

An island is land with water all around it. Islands may be large, like Greenland, or very small, like Manhattan. Some islands are in rivers or lakes, and some are in oceans.

This island is in Lake Titicaca, in South America.

The Thousand Islands are part of the Saint Lawrence River.

Islands in oceans may be mountaintops sticking up above the water. The Hawaiian Islands are examples of this kind of mountaintop. In warm seas, there are islands made out of **coral**.

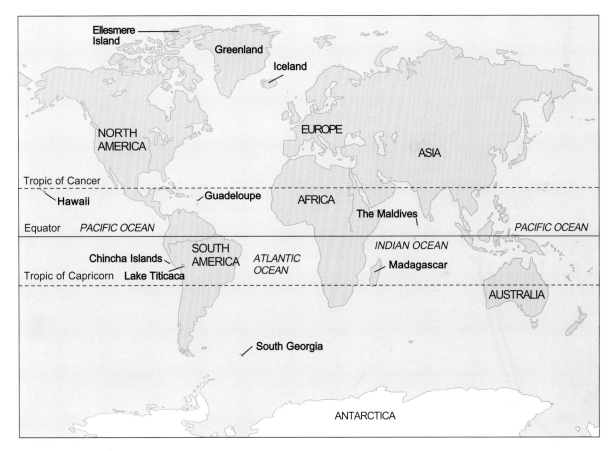

On this map, you can see the names of the islands that you will read about in this book.

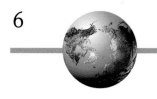

Life on Islands

Some islands are a long way from any other land areas. We call them remote islands. It may take days, or weeks, to reach remote islands by boat.

Small aircraft carry people and goods to and from some remote islands. This aircraft is on Ellesmere Island in the Arctic Ocean.

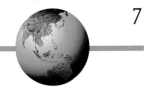

Many islanders catch and sell fish for a living. There are often fishing villages, or fishing **ports**, on island coasts.

This fishing harbor is on the coast of Iceland. The seas around Iceland are rich in fish, such as herring and cod. Icelanders **export**, or sell, fish to other countries.

Many of the world's islands are vacation resorts. The resorts bring tourists to the islands, and this helps the island people to earn money.

This beach is on the Caribbean island of Guadeloupe.

Before people settled, or went to live, on some islands, very few animals lived there. People brought in animals such as rats, dogs, pigs, and cows.

Plant seeds are carried to islands by the wind, the ocean, or birds. Birds usually nest in places where they are safe from both people and animals.

This is one of the Chincha Islands off the coast of Peru. Brown pelicans nest here every year.

Madagascar

Madagascar is a large, **tropical** island off the east coast of Africa. It has many different **habitats**. There are forests, deserts, grasslands, and high mountains.

Plants and animals on the island have

This farmer in Madagascar uses oxen to pull his plow.

developed differently from those in Africa. These changes took place over hundreds of millions of years.

Some plants and animals here are not found anywhere else in the world. There are special **preserves** and **national parks** where they are **protected**.

The island has many kinds of lemurs, like the ring-tailed lemur. There are many snake families and many kinds of reptiles. One of the rarest turtles of all is found here.

Emperor moths, like this one, live on the island.

Baobab trees grow in Madagascar. They are well **adapted** to dry places. They store water in their trunks, which swell and look like giant bottles.

This baobab tree is growing in southwest Madagascar.

The baobab trees have many uses. People make rope and cloth from the bark and make paper from the wood.

Nearly 12 million people live on the island of Madagascar. They need land for cattle and to grow **crops** to eat and to sell. Coffee, vanilla, and cloves are grown on the island.

The people have cleared forest habitats to make farmland. Many forest animals and plants are in danger and may die out in about 50 years.

On Madagascar a woman is herding her ducks. You can see the rice fields behind her.

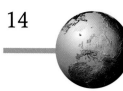

Iceland

Iceland is an island country near the Arctic.
Deep below the ground here, the rocks are hot.
These hot rocks heat water under the ground.

In some places, the hot water blows up out of the
ground. This spray of steam and hot water is a
geyser. You can see geysers in the picture.

Pipes carry hot water into people's homes, where they use it for cooking and washing. Hot water also heats greenhouses where people grow fruits and vegetables.

Hot water also flows slowly out of the ground to form pools. In this picture, people are relaxing in a hot pool. The power plant behind the swimmers uses hot water to produce electricity.

Reykjavik is the capital city of Iceland. Most of Iceland's 270,300 people live there and in other cities along the coast. A main road runs all around the island. It links the villages and towns to the capital city.

Only a small part of the land is used for growing crops. Farmers raise sheep for their meat, wool, and milk. Many people in

You can see that Reykjavik is on the coast.

Iceland make their living from the sea. Fishing is the most important industry.

Before people settled in Iceland, only one kind of **mammal** lived there. This was the Arctic fox. Now, there are wild reindeer and mink, as well as farm animals such as cows and sheep. No **reptiles** live on Iceland, but there are many kinds of ducks and other birds, too.

Some of the birds, such as this gyrfalcon, are not often seen outside Iceland.

The Maldives

The Maldives is a country of more than 1,000 small islands in the Indian Ocean. The islands are low and flat and are all made of coral.

This is the Kaafa Atoll in the Maldives.

People live on 200 of the islands. Coconut palms and other trees and plants cover most of the Maldive Islands. People grow fruit, such as papayas and pineapples.

There is not enough space or soil to grow other food crops. However, the ocean around the islands is full of fish. Many kinds of fish, such as the bonito, tuna, and swordfish, are plentiful here.

The islanders catch fish from wooden sailing boats.

Seventy of the Maldive Islands are **vacation resorts**. The houses on these islands are built specially for visitors to stay in. People like to swim in the warm ocean and dive to see the corals and fish.

Tourists enjoy the hot, sunny weather and the beautiful beaches on the islands.

The world's weather is changing because of **global warming**. Some scientists think the sea level may rise by up to 15 inches (38 cm) in the next 40 years. This would drown many Maldive Islands.

If these scientists are right, the people of Maldives may soon have to leave their homes. Even so, scientists are not sure what will happen in the future.

The coral islands in this picture may one day be below the ocean.

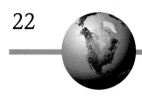

Hawaii

Hawaii is the largest of the Hawaiian Islands in the Pacific Ocean. There are two active **volcanoes** on Hawaii, Mauna Loa and Kilauea. Both are in Volcanoes National Park.

Red hot **lava** pours out of volcanoes when they explode.

The island of Hawaii has many different habitats. There are mountains, old lava flows, rain forests, deserts, grasslands, and sandy beaches.

There are many different plants and birds. Hawaii is famous for its hibiscus flowers and the Hawaiian goose. This goose was saved from becoming **extinct**, or dying out.

The Hawaiian goose, or nene (NAY–nay), lives high up in the hills and mountains of Hawaii.

Hawaii is a very popular vacation spot. There are vacation resorts around the coast of Hawaii. In summer, when the weather is hot and sunny, the beaches are crowded with vacationers.

People visit the Volcanoes National Park to

Tourists enjoy watching Hawaiian dances.

see the volcanoes and the wildlife that lives there. In winter, tourists ski in the snow-covered mountains.

Most of the land on Hawaii is used for growing crops to export to other countries. Farmers grow coffee, nuts, cotton, and tropical fruits for export. When farmers clear the land, plants and animals lose their habitats.

This picture shows fields where pineapples are growing.

South Georgia

South Georgia is a small, remote island in the South Atlantic Ocean. There is snow and ice during the whole year.

The only people who live on South Georgia are scientists. Here they are diving from a boat to study sea life.

The main plants on the island are lichens, mosses, and tussock grass. It is too cold and snowy for trees or flowering plants to grow there.

Insects live in the grass. They are food for small birds such as the pipit. The pipit is the only songbird that lives this far south.

Seabirds nest on South Georgia. The bird in this picture is a gray-headed albatross.

Many different kinds of seals and penguins live on South Georgia. These animals eat fish from the ocean. Seals have their young on this bleak island.

This is a male elephant seal. Its long nose looks like an elephant's trunk.

In 1904, whale hunters set up whaling stations on the island. They brought rats and reindeer with them, and the island habitat changed.

The hunters killed fur seals as well as whales in the seas around the island. These animals almost died out, or became extinct.

Today, hunting is not allowed. Whaling stations like the one in this picture are no longer used.

Glossary

adapted: If a plant or an animal can find everything it needs to live in a place, we say it has adapted to that place. The animals can find food and shelter, and the plants have enough food in the soil and enough water. Some animals have changed their shape or their color over a long time, so that they can catch food or hide easily. Some plants in dry areas can store water in their stems or roots.

coral: A small sea creature. Some corals have hard casings, or skeletons. These form a kind of rock, also called coral.

crops: Plants that farmers grow to use or to sell.

export: Sell and take to another country.

extinct: No longer exists on Earth. This plant or animal has died out.

geyser: Spring of steam and hot water that is forced out of the ground into the air.

global warming: The warming up of the weather all around the world.

habitats: The natural homes of plants or animals. Examples of habitats are deserts, forests, and wetlands.

lava: Very hot, melted rock that flows out of a volcano. It comes from deep in the Earth up to the surface.

mammal: One of a group of animals whose young feed on their mother's milk.

national parks: Laws protect these lands and their wildlife from harm. These places usually have beautiful scenery and rare wildlife.

ports: Towns where ships load and unload their goods.

preserves: Areas set aside for wildlife to live in safely.

protected: Kept safe from changes that would damage the habitat.

reptiles: A group of animals that includes snakes and lizards.

tropical: Places that are hot and wet all year are called tropical.

vacation resorts: Villages or towns that people visit for vacations.

volcanoes: Hills or mountains made when lava is blown up or pours out of the Earth.

Index